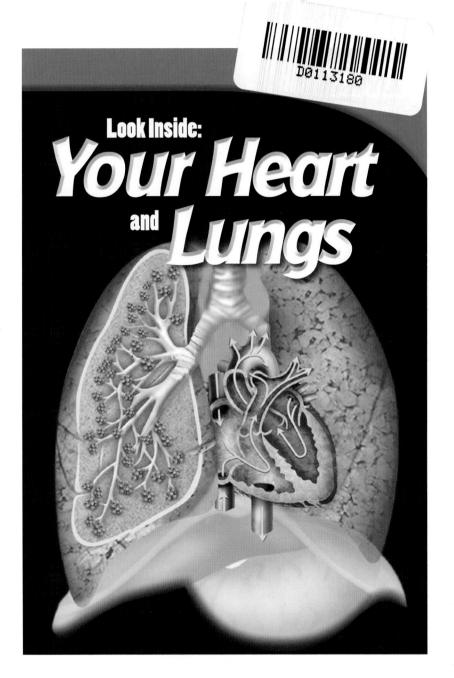

Look Inside:
Your Heart
and *Lungs*

Ben Williams

Consultant

Timothy Rasinski, Ph.D.
Kent State University

Publishing Credits

Dona Herweck Rice, *Editor-in-Chief*
Robin Erickson, *Production Director*
Lee Aucoin, *Creative Director*
Conni Medina, M.A.Ed., *Editorial Director*
Jamey Acosta, *Editor*
Stephanie Reid, *Photo Editor*
Rachelle Cracchiolo, M.S.Ed., *Publisher*

Image Credits

Cover illustration by Rick Nease; p.4 top: Olinchuk/Shutterstock; p.4 bottom: Pavzyk Svitlana/Shutterstock; p.5 Monkey Business Images/Shutterstock; p.6 ArtisticCaptures/iStockphoto; p.7 Rick Nease; p.8 top: Anton Balazh/Shutterstock; p.8 Morris Huberland/Science Source/Photo Researchers; p.9 top: Alila Sao Mai/Shutterstock; p.9 bottom: abimages/Shutterstock ; p.10 sjlocke/iStockphoto; p.12 top: sjlocke/iStockphoto; p.12 bottom: Olinchuk/Shutterstock; p.13 Arstudio/Shutterstock; p.16 Rob Marmion/Shutterstock; p.16 Rob Marmion/Shutterstock; p.17 bottom: Alex Mit/Shutterstock; p.18 Sebastian Kaulitzki/Shutterstock; p.19 Video Surgery/Photo Researchers; p.20 CEFutcher/iStockphoto; p.21 back: Sebastian Kaulitzki/Shutterstock; p.22 yenwen/iStockphoto; p.24 strmko/iStockphoto; p.25 totophotos/Shutterstock; p.27 bottom: gbh007/iStockphoto; p.28 martan/Shutterstock; back cover Sebastian Kaulitzki/Shutterstock

Based on writing from *TIME For Kids.*

TIME For Kids and the *TIME For Kids* logo are registered trademarks of TIME Inc. Used under license.

Teacher Created Materials

5301 Oceanus Drive
Huntington Beach, CA 92649-1030
http://www.tcmpub.com

ISBN 978-1-4333-3636-2

© 2012 Teacher Created Materials, Inc.
Made in China
Nordica.122017.CA21701270

Table of Contents

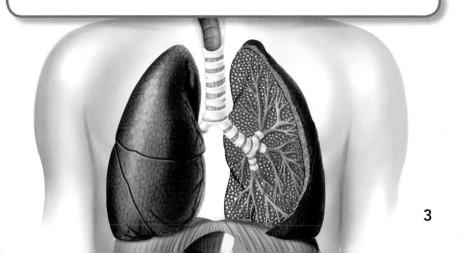

A Busy Place

The world is a busy place. People work, play, and go, go, go! Over here and over there, something is always happening.

The outside world is very busy. But there is another busy world, one that you

can't see. Inside of you, under your skin, your body never stops going. **Blood** goes through your body. Air goes in and out. Yes, your *inside* world is very busy, too!

An Important Team

In the middle of all this activity, your heart and lungs are resting snugly inside your chest. They are an important team! They work together every moment of every day to send your body the **oxygen** and nutrition it needs. They take good care of you, so you must be sure to take good care of them!

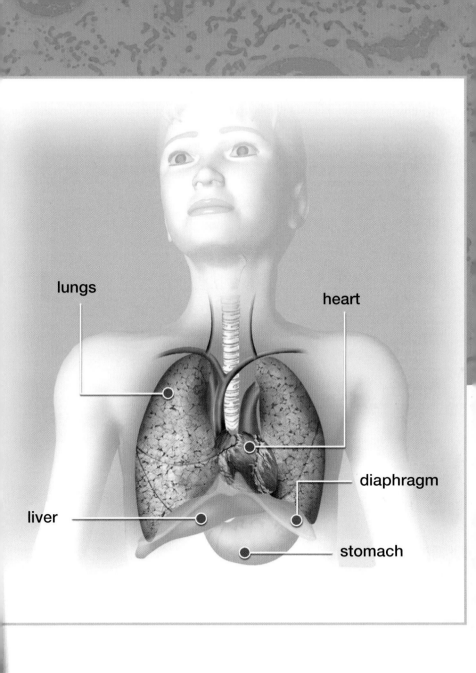

lungs

heart

liver

diaphragm

stomach

The Heart and How It Works

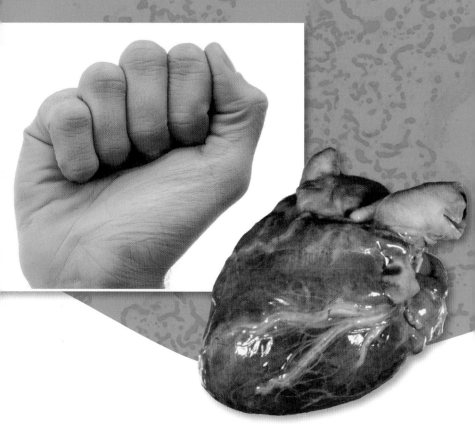

Your heart is in your chest, between your lungs and just left of the center. It is about the size of a closed fist.

How Blood Moves

Blood travels from your heart to all parts of your body through your arteries. Blood returns to your heart through your veins.

People sometimes think a heart is the shape of a valentine. A real heart looks nothing like that.

9

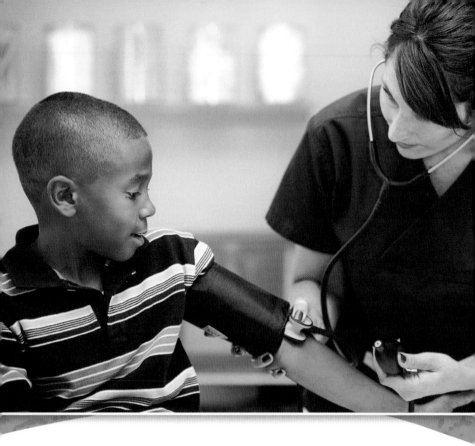

Your heart pumps blood through your body. Blood brings oxygen to your body's **cells**. Living things need oxygen or they will die. Once your cells receive the oxygen, the blood returns to your heart to get more. Then your blood is pumped out again.

Heartbeats

Did you know that your heart beats about 100,000 times a day? It just keeps beating on its own. You do not have to think about it to make it happen.

Blood Pressure

When you go to the doctor, the nurse will check your blood pressure using a stethoscope and a blood pressure cuff. High blood pressure could lead to serious health problems, such as heart failure or a stroke.

In and out, in and out: that is how your heart pumps your blood.

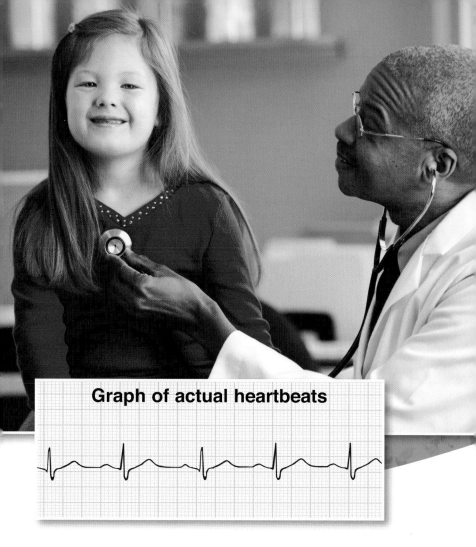

Graph of actual heartbeats

Place your hand over your heart. Do you feel something? It is your heartbeat. Your heart beats as it pumps the blood.

Listen to Your Heart

It is difficult to place your ear against your chest to hear your heartbeat. So you can use a stethoscope. A stethoscope is a special instrument with two ear pieces connected to a long tube and a flat piece at the end. If the flat piece is held against your chest and the ear pieces are placed in your ears, you can hear your heartbeat very clearly.

Your heart beats in a pattern of two. If you heard the sound of your heartbeat, the first beat would sound dull and the second beat would sound sharp. It would sound like this: thump THUMP, thump THUMP.

How does your heart work? Look at the diagram. Blood enters your heart from your lungs. Your heart pumps the blood into your **arteries**. Once the oxygen is delivered, your **veins** carry the blood back to your heart. The blood then goes into your lungs for a fresh supply of oxygen.

lung

heart

Circulation

Your heart is like a pump that moves blood through your body every second of every day. This is called *circulation*.

lung

A body can't work well with a sick heart. You must take good care of your heart to keep your whole body strong. Exercising every day and eating right can help your heart stay healthy.

The Lungs and How They Work

Your two lungs are in your chest on either side of your heart. They look like soft, wet, pink-gray sponges.

Breathe in deeply and you can see your chest rise. That is because your lungs are filling with air. Breathe out and your chest lowers.
It is releasing the air.

Breathing
Just like with your heartbeat, you do not need to think about breathing. Your body just breathes on its own.

left lung
outside

left lung
inside

Why do you need to breathe? You breathe to get oxygen. You breathe air into your nose and down your **trachea** (TREY-kee-uh). Your trachea carries the air through tubes that look like the branches of an upside-down tree. The tubes are called **bronchi** (BRONG-key). They take the oxygen from the air and send it to your blood.

Your body knows how much air it needs. If you run hard or get scared, you will breathe faster to get more oxygen.

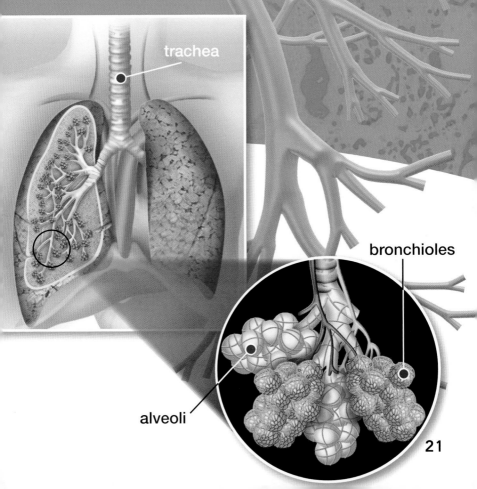

How We Breathe

Your trachea is also called a *windpipe*. Your bronchi look like two long branches. They break into smaller branches called bronchioles (BRONG-key-ohls). At the ends of the bronchioles are tiny air sacks called alveoli (al-VEE-uh-li).

trachea

bronchioles

alveoli

21

When you breathe, your nose and lungs work together to moisten, warm, and clean the air. Your lungs only want pure, fresh oxygen.

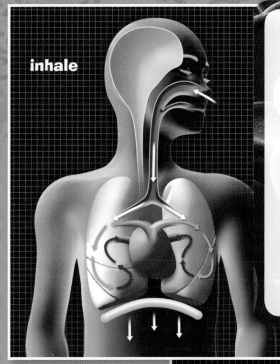

inhale

Inhale

You inhale (breathe in) to get oxygen into your body. You exhale (breathe out) to get rid of gases, like carbon dioxide, that you do not need. When you inhale, the muscles around your lungs pull your lungs down. This makes the lungs bigger inside and lets them suck in air.

Exhale

When you exhale, your muscles relax and your lungs go back to their normal size. This forces the gases out of your body.

exhale

Since there is oxygen in water, why can fish breathe underwater but we can't? Sharks and fish have gills that take oxygen from the water for them. We do not have gills. We can only get our oxygen from the air or with the help of special equipment, such as a scuba tank.

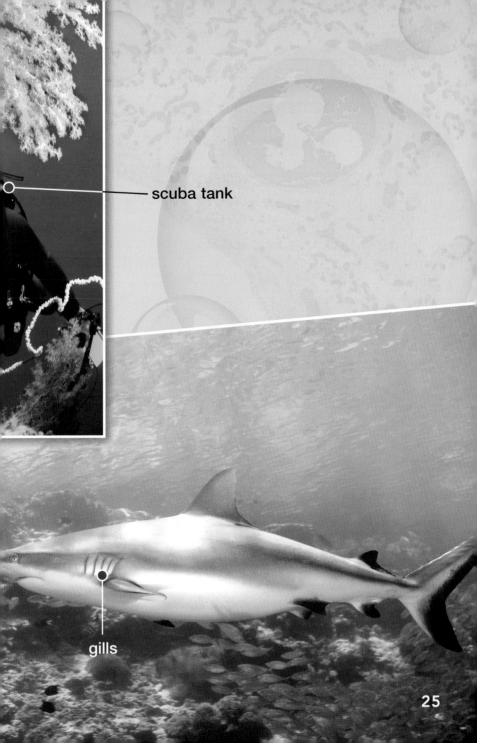

scuba tank

gills

Healthy Heart and Lungs

What can you do to take good care of your heart and lungs? Here are some important things to remember to keep them healthy and strong:

- Eat right. Healthy food means a healthy heart and lungs.

- Exercise every day. It keeps your heart and lungs strong.

- Get plenty of rest. Rest helps your heart and lungs get the energy they need.

- See your doctor for check-ups, then you can be sure that your heart and lungs are well.

- Be happy! A good attitude helps to keep your heart and lungs healthy.

- Do not smoke! Smoking damages your heart and lungs and makes them work much too hard.

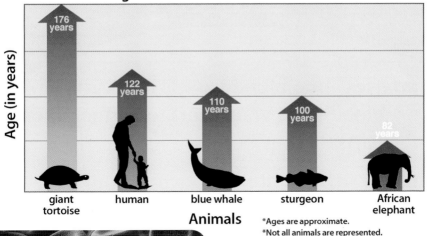

Age of the Oldest-Known Animals

Age (in years)

giant tortoise — 176 years
human — 122 years
blue whale — 110 years
sturgeon — 100 years
African elephant — 82 years

Animals

*Ages are approximate.
*Not all animals are represented.

A Long Life

Here is a graph to show the age for the oldest-known animals. When you take good care of your heart and lungs, you help yourself to live a long time. You might even live to be 122!

Glossary

arteries—the blood vessels that carry blood from your heart to all the other parts of your body

blood—the fluid that moves through the body's veins and arteries

bronchi—the two main branches of the trachea

cells—one of the tiny units that are the basic building blocks of living things

circulation—the movement of blood through your body that is powered by your heart

oxygen—a gas that is necessary for life

trachea—the main part of the system of tubes by which air passes to and from the lungs

veins—the vessel that brings blood back to your heart